TIME TRAVELERS

ICE MAIDEN
OF THE ANDES

Janet Buell

Twenty-First Century Books

Brookfield, Connecticut

Twenty-First Century Books
A Division of The Millbrook Press
2 Old New Milford Road
Brookfield, CT 06804

Library of Congress Cataloging-in-Publication Data
Buell, Janet.
Ice maiden of the Andes/Janet Buell.
p. cm.
Includes bibliographical references and index.
Summary: Discusses the discovery of the 500-year-old frozen body of a young girl on
a mountaintop in the Andes and how this discovery has increased our knowledge
of the ancient South American civilization of the Incas.
1. Incas—Funeral customs and rites—Juvenile literature. 2. Incas—Religion—Juvenile literature.
3. Incas—Antiquities—Juvenile literature. 4. Mummies—Peru—Ampato, Mount—Juvenile literature. 5. Excavations (Archaeology)—Peru—Ampato, Mount—Juvenile literature. 6. Ampato, Mount
(Peru)—Antiquities—Juvenile literature. [1. Incas—Antiquities. 2. Indians of South America—
Antiquities. 3. Excavations (Archaeology)—Peru. 4. Archaeology. 5. Peru—Antiquities.]
F3429.3.F85B84   1997   97-23372
985'.32—dc21   CIP
                                                                                 AC

ISBN 0-8050-5185-6

Designed by Kelly Soong
Map by Jeffrey L. Ward

Printed in the United States of America

3   5   7   9   10   8   6   4   2

Photo Credits

Cover: © Johan Reinhard. pp. 8, 20: © Stephen L. Alvarez/National Geographic Society Image Sales;
pp. 9, 23, 25: © William J. Conklin; pp. 11, 17, 18, 21, 41, 49: © Johan Reinhard; p. 15: © Paul
Hanny/Gamma Liaison; p. 27: © Maria Stenzel/National Geographic Society Images Sales; pp. 31,
48: © Corbis-Bettmann; p. 33 (top): © The Granger Collection; pp. 33 (bottom), 34 (right), 43: Loren
McIntyre/Woodfin Camp; p. 34 (left): © Douglas Mason/Woodfin Camp; p. 35: © Wolfgang
Kaehler/Gamma Liaison; p. 39: © Robert Frerck/Woodfin Camp; p. 46: © H. Silvester/Rapho/Gamma
Liaison.

To my nephew, Cody Buell,
who loves all the mysteries of the world

ACKNOWLEDGMENTS

Many thanks to textile expert Bill Conklin and archaeologist Johan Reinhard. A special thanks to Liesl Clark, producer of Web pages for PBS's *Nova*, who has been very generous with her time and resources. As always, a very big thank you to my editor, Pat Culleton, for her wisdom, guidance, and good humor.

CONTENTS

ONE   Mountain Discovery   7

TWO   Archaeology at Altitude   14

THREE   Ancient Evidence   22

FOUR   Sun Gods and Sacrifice   29

FIVE   Mountain Gods and Mummies   38

SIX   Last Days   45

TIMELINE   Mummies of the Inca   51

Glossary   53

Source Notes   57

Further Reading   59

Index   61

BRAZIL

PERU

Lima

Cuzco

Sara Sara *Mount Ampato*

Mount Sabancaya

Arequipa

Lake Titicaca

La Paz BOLIVIA

Sajama

Tata Sabaya

Pacific Ocean

CHILE

PARAGUAY

Mount Copiapó

ARGENTINA

A N D E S   M O U N T A I N S

Mount Aconcagua

El Plomo

Santiago

URUGUAY

Buenos Aires

N

0   250   500 Miles

0   250   500 Kilometers

Atlantic Ocean

ONE

MOUNTAIN

DISCOVERY

Johan Reinhard had never seen anything like it before. Acres of ice pinnacles, most of them taller than a man, spiked the upper slopes of Mount Ampato. At 20,700 feet, Ampato should have been covered by a thick sheet of ice. But now, Reinhard's boots crunched on the slope's gravelly surface as he and his climbing partner, Miguel Zárate, made their way through the forest of ice-blue spires. In the distance, smoke spewed from the cone of Mount Sabancaya's crater.

The volcano was the reason Reinhard and Zárate had climbed Peru's Ampato in the first place. They thought it would be perfect for watching Sabancaya's dusty plume rising a mile into the sky. Instead, they found the changes on Ampato itself even more interesting. Zárate's brother reported that when he had climbed it two years earlier in 1993, a thick layer of ice topped the summit. He also told them the summit ridge was at least 30 feet wide. Now it was less than 3 feet. In two years, the volcano had changed everything. As black ash rained down on Ampato, it covered the mountain's icy surface. The dark particles absorbed sunlight, creating a melt that helped form the icy spires and caused the summit ridge to collapse.

As they neared the peak, Zárate went on ahead while Reinhard stopped to take notes. Soon, a whistle from Zárate interrupted him. He looked up to see his companion waving his ice ax in a motion that meant Reinhard should hurry. When

Climbers work their way through the ice spires at 20,700 feet on Mount Ampato in the Andes of Peru. Smoke from the Mount Sabancaya volcano is in the background.

he reached Zárate, the man pointed down a steep slope to where red feathers stuck out of the mountain's black surface.

Zárate volunteered to descend the slope to get a closer look. They secured a rope around his waist, and with Reinhard holding on tightly to the other end, the climber sidestepped his way down the steep incline. As his fingers brushed away dirt around the feathers, he could see they crowned a small figure made of gold and spondylus shell. Prodding the cold soil further, he found two more figures, one of gold and one of silver. Each wore a feathered headdress.[1]

The Inca brought spondylus shells from the ocean. They thought this shell represented the ocean goddess.

This small figure was found in 1995 near the summit of Mount Ampato.

The men knew there was only one reason for the statuettes to be on the mountaintop. This was one of the sacred sites of the Inca, a nation of people whose empire once stretched 2,500 miles along the Andes mountains of South America. It was here that Inca priests offered up things to please their mountain gods: figurines, pottery, textiles, food, and drink. It was here, too, that the Inca offered their most precious gift to the powerful gods—their children.

Returning to the summit, Reinhard and Zárate discovered two boulder walls. The walls had once formed part of a rectangular ceremonial platform the Inca had built more than 500 years ago at a high point on Ampato. When the summit collapsed, part of the platform tumbled down the slope.

They looked down into the ravines that dropped 200 feet below them. If anything remained of the Inca sacrifices, they were somewhere down there. But the ravines stretched out in a vast expanse of gray rubble and ice. From where the men stood, they could not see if any sacrificial remains lay within them. Without knowing the route the platform took, a search would probably take hours or days. To quicken the task, Reinhard took two sheets of bright yellow plastic from his climber's pack and tied each around a large rock. Standing at the ridge near the platform, he tossed them down the slope.

Ascending to higher ground, the two climbers peered down into the ravines. Finally, they spied the yellow bundles. Near them lay what appeared to be another bundle of brown cloth. To stop their hopes from soaring, they told each other that perhaps it was just the lost backpack of a modern-day climber.

As they carefully descended the gravel-strewn slope that September 1995 day, the men could see the rough cloth more clearly. When they got closer, they grew more excited as they realized that it wasn't a climber's backpack after all. It was a mummy bundle, or *fardo,* as the Peruvians call it. Reinhard, an archaeologist who has climbed more than 100 Andean peaks—more than any other man—had never before seen a mummy bundle like this on a mountain.

The fardo lay partially frozen in an icy outcropping. Around it, artifacts littered the ground: a tiny female figure made of spondylus shell, pieces of pottery, llama bones, and bits of cloth. The men also found two small cloth bags containing corn kernels and a corn cob.

The fardo had tumbled from a great height, and they had no idea if the mummy inside it had survived the fall. Zárate carefully chopped at the ice around it. After he chopped partway through, he turned the bundle on its side. Suddenly, they found themselves looking into the empty eyesockets of a young girl, her mouth open in a grim, but peaceful, smile. Sun and the mountain wind had dried her head, but when they lifted her body, the weight of ice within it told them her body had remained frozen.[2]

A Tough Decision

As Zárate and Reinhard looked at the Inca girl, they realized the significance of the bundle they held in their hands. They knew from the statuettes they found with her that the girl was at least 500 years old. The fact that she was frozen was a lucky break. Most naturally made mummies are dried out, which affects the amount of information we can learn from them. Scientists can more easily study the viruses and bacteria that live within frozen tissue. And they can extract DNA, the sub-

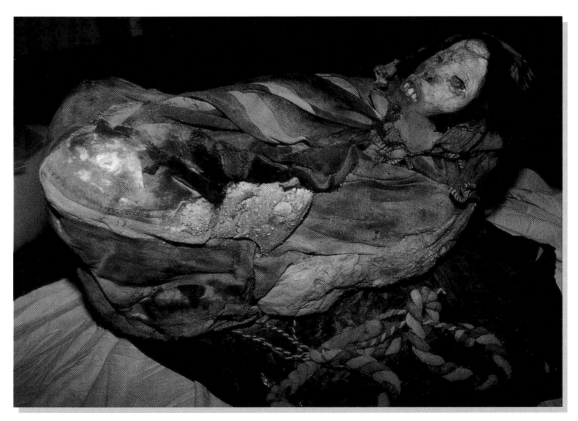

Ice is still visible on this 500-year-old mummy of a young Inca girl. Because it was frozen and not dried out, scientists can learn about the viruses and bacteria that live in the mummy's frozen tissue. This ice maiden came to be called Juanita.

stance in cells that passes from parent to child, giving them their familial characteristics.

The men faced a tough decision. Left on the mountaintop, the young girl's body faced certain damage from the volcanic ash sweeping down on her from Sabancaya. Theft was a risk, too. Even the difficulty of climbing hadn't kept looters and treasure seekers from the tops of other sacred mountains, where they used dynamite to break a peak's icy hold on its artifacts. And there was always the threat that snow would fall on the mountaintop, burying the young girl again.

Then, too, they had to consider what it would mean to bring her down. The climb off the mountain would be difficult and long. In the three days from the mountain summit to the freezers at Catholic University in Arequipa, the young girl's body could defrost. If that happened, scientists and archaeologists would lose a precious opportunity to learn more about her.

Reinhard and Zárate decided to bring her down.

They knew they had to act quickly. Night was coming on and snow had begun to fall. Though Reinhard suffered from a stomach ailment, he decided he would carry the 80-pound bundle to their mountain camp 1,500 feet below. They transferred Reinhard's personal camping gear from his expedition pack to Zárate's. After wrapping the young girl in a plastic sheet, they tied her to the pack.

As they descended the mountain, the sun slid lower in the sky. With almost every step, Reinhard slipped on the ash-covered slope. On the steepest parts, Zárate cut steps into the slope with his ice ax. With the sun descending faster than they were, it was a dangerously slow journey. Zárate begged Reinhard to leave the mummy behind. He knew that one false step by Reinhard might send all three of them sliding uncontrollably down the mountain.

Finally, Reinhard relented, and they unloaded the Inca maiden from his back. They wedged her between two ice pinnacles and continued their descent. In the dark, their headlamps illuminated little of the steep mountainside. It took them another two hours to get to their high camp.

The next morning, with a new rain of ash falling from Sabancaya, Reinhard returned to the mummy while Zárate carried their gear down to the base camp at 16,300 feet. Then he returned to help Reinhard. By late afternoon, the men finally arrived at the base camp. Fearing that the body would defrost at these warmer elevations, they wrapped her in their two sleeping bags and hoped it would keep the body insulated and cold. The burro driver met them at camp and helped them load the mummy onto the back of his animal.

The men walked for thirteen hours to the nearest village, Cabanaconde. There they loaded the girl onto the overnight bus to Arequipa. With Zárate as her traveling companion and Reinhard following on a later bus with the artifacts, the Inca ice maiden made her quiet entry into the twentieth century. Sixty-four hours after discovery, her body had stayed frozen within the sleeping bags. Within days, scientists would begin the task of unraveling her ancient secrets.[3]

T W O

ARCHAEOLOGY

AT ALTITUDE

For five hundred years the young Inca girl lay peacefully beneath her blanket of snow and ice. Now, as she returned to the modern world, news of her discovery spread quickly around the globe. For the second time in a few years, an ancient human had been found at one of the world's highest elevations. The first was Ice Man, a traveler who died more than 5,000 years ago in the Alps, a mountain range on the border of Switzerland and Italy. Hikers discovered Ice Man's freeze-dried corpse in 1991 after desert sandstorms in Africa swept dust into the air over Europe. The dust landed on the mountain, where it warmed the thickly frozen glacial topping. Weapons discovered with Ice Man revealed that neolithic people were much more advanced than we had previously believed.[1]

The Inca civilization in South America disappeared after the Spanish conquistadors invaded the empire in 1532. Though the Inca were eventually absorbed into the Spanish culture, they left behind evidence of their way of life, including many artifacts. But artifacts don't tell the whole story. And the history of the Inca as recorded by the Spanish tends to be biased against the culture the Spanish conquered. Scientists hoped that by studying an ancient in-the-flesh Inca, they could learn more about her people.

When she arrived at Catholic University in Arequipa, Peru, scientists set about the difficult task of trying to keep the young girl, whom they now called Juanita,

*Ice Man, frozen in a glacier for more than 5,000 years,
was found in 1991. He lived during the Bronze Age.*

from defrosting. Archaeologists find so few frozen bodies that each one represents a new challenge when it comes to investigating it properly. If they didn't make the right decisions regarding her care, it was possible they could damage Juanita and her clothing, and lose valuable information about her past.[2]

RETURN TO MOUNT AMPATO

While the scientists struggled with their dilemma, Reinhard planned a return expedition to Ampato's 20,700-foot summit. On their first trip, he and Zárate had discovered more evidence of the Inca on Ampato. Reinhard knew there were even more secrets to be revealed at the high altitude. And he knew he'd have to find them before it snowed again. Quickly, he assembled an eighteen-member archaeological team to make a second assault.

Four-mile-high archaeology presents special challenges unlike any faced by archaeologists at lower altitudes. Reinhard was no stranger to the challenge. He has excavated high mountain sites in both the Andes and Himalayas, the highest mountain range in the world.

Distance complicates any expedition in the Andes. There are few major cities near the mountain range, and no superhighways lead to the mountains. Roads aren't always kept in the best condition either. They may be washed out or blocked by rock falls or simply full of potholes. Buses in the South American countryside may be unreliable due to poor upkeep and age. Expedition members may board an ancient bus that tends to break down every few hours. If the bus is too overloaded, it may have trouble climbing even the smallest hill. Then, passengers have to get out and push.

The closest drop-off point is usually miles away from the mountain. The scientists unload their archaeological equipment, food, and personal gear and strap it onto the backs of llamas, burros, or humans hired to carry it to the mountain. The next leg of the journey, the hike to a base camp, can sometimes take two days or more.

Once the ascent begins, life for the climbers changes drastically. As they go higher, the air gets thinner. At our usual altitude, air presses against us at 15 pounds per square inch. Three of those pounds are made up of oxygen. At higher altitudes that amount drops. Work at high altitudes is made more difficult by this lack of oxygen, called hypoxia. Even during sleep, hypoxia makes it hard to breathe, and the archaeologists find themselves waking up often as they gasp for breath.

Climbers are constantly tired from lack of sleep and oxygen. All this deep

Pack animals are an important part of high-altitude climbs. Mules, burros, or llamas carry loads of equipment and supplies to base camps at different altitudes.

breathing causes a climber to lose water vapor, so he or she has to drink lots of water to keep hydrated. In severe cases, hypoxia and dehydration can cause muddled thinking, a dangerous condition at such heights. Headaches, too, are a natural part of high-altitude climbing, along with nausea, lack of appetite, and other ailments.

Then there's the danger of unpredictable mountain weather. Besides the high winds and numbing cold, there is always the possibility that a thunderstorm will catch a climber unawares on the mountain. Many climbers have been killed by lightning strikes. On another mountain ascent Reinhard himself was knocked unconscious when lightning struck nearby. Now he retreats to lower altitudes when skies threaten a storm.

At normal altitudes, archaeologists generally excavate carefully, using trowels and brushes. But at high altitudes, time is one luxury the diggers don't have. Pick-axes and shovels quicken excavation time, and every minute counts. During one excavation on Mount Copiapó in Chile, it took Reinhard's six-person team twelve

*Anthropologist Johan Reinhard, one of the men who found the
ice maiden mummy, excavating a site at 19,300 feet on Mount Ampato.*

days to excavate a 26-foot by 13-foot platform buried in 6 feet of frozen ground. Bone-piercing cold and high winds further hampered their progress.[3]

HIGH-ALTITUDE PIONEERS

On their first trip to Ampato, Reinhard and Zárate caught glimpses of the elaborate preparations the Inca had made for their assault. Now the two men and their team could get a close-up view of those preparations. The evidence showed that modern-day climbers weren't the first to invent high-mountain climbing techniques.

Today, high-mountain climbers establish camps at the base of the mountains they climb. The Inca thought of these base camps, too, and they also established other camps along the line of ascent just as modern climbers do. The ancient climbers went even further. Along the route, they constructed camps where they and their pack animals could rest. Reinhard and his team discovered the remains of wooden posts embedded in the ground and low rock walls—remains of their blanket-covered tents. The Inca also built stone corrals for their llamas, which they used as pack animals. Today some of these corrals are ankle-deep with the animals' droppings.[4]

On their first trip, Reinhard and Zárate discovered areas of ice formations streaked with wild grass, called *ichu*. They knew wild grass doesn't grow at such high elevations. It was clear the Inca had transported it to the mountaintop from below. Now, on their return journey, they saw the extent of the Inca efforts. Hundreds of square yards of ichu covered acres of the mountainside. The Inca had hauled it up the mountain to insulate their tent floors and to carpet the trail to the summit. It must have meant hundreds of trips from below.[5]

TWO MORE BODIES

On this second trip, Reinhard's team found two more grave sites below Juanita's. Within the first lay the body of what scientists would later determine to be a young boy. A small, silver male figure lay buried with him. As they uncovered the body, they could see he had been struck by lightning in his grave. This reduced him to charred bones and burned bits of clothing. The heat of the lightning was so intense a pottery jug buried with the boy fused to the earth. Oddly enough, a pair of wooden cups buried with him remained unharmed by the lightning bolt.

The other tomb presented a more difficult challenge. After digging through a top layer of ash, the archaeologists came to a surprising layer of frozen red earth. They knew the Inca gave great significance to the color red. Other Inca sacrifices bore evidence of red paint on their skin, and the Inca often painted their faces red during important ceremonies. Like the ichu, red earth doesn't occur naturally at that elevation. This meant the Inca also transported it from below. Beneath this layer of red earth they discovered a frozen layer of rock and gravel. It was in this layer that the body was embedded.

Before they could remove the body, the archaeologists needed to melt its shroud of frozen earth. At this height, the task seemed impossible. They tried using a blowtorch to melt the sides of the tomb, but the rock and gravel made it impossibly slow. Next they used boiling water and poured it over the sides of the grave. Bare fingers picked away the slowly melting ice from the body. The cold and wet conditions caused painful cracks in the skin of their fingers. It took three days of heating, pouring, and picking to break the grave's icy hold.

These wooden cups were found with the body of a young Inca boy at another grave site high on Mount Ampato, but below the ice maiden site.

When they finally freed it, the archaeologists lifted a young girl's body from its 500-year-old grave. By the size of the mummy bundle, the scientists could tell she had been quite young when sacrificed to the mountain god, perhaps no more than eight years old. She wore an elaborate feather headdress, the first the archaeologists had seen on a sacrificial mummy. Scientists theorize the girl's sacrificers may have had trouble fitting her into the grave. When they buried her, they simply pushed down on her head, crushing the headdress, to make her fit better. Scientists later found that a lightning strike had also damaged the young girl's body.

Her tomb held things she most needed in the afterlife: wooden drinking vessels, spoons, weaving tools, and offering bundles, which she would have given as presents to the gods. The archaeologists also found a tiny pair of sandals made from plant fibers and alpaca straps, a grim reminder that this had once been a living, breathing little girl.

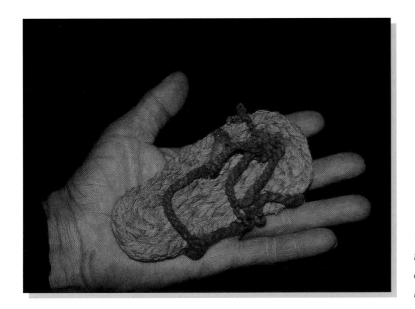

This tiny sandal belonged to an Inca child sacrificed centuries ago and was buried with her.

Reinhard discovered the grave sites of the young children at 19,200 feet, some 1,500 feet below Juanita's grave site. This fact might mean they were of lesser importance than the ice maiden and perhaps were sent as servants for the ice maiden in her afterlife. The pair of young children faced south, a direction the Inca may have associated with death. The two may have been buried as a symbolic marriage. One Spanish chronicler, Juan de Betanzos, wrote that "Many boys and girls were sacrificed in pairs, being buried alive and well dressed and adorned. With each pair they buried . . . items that a married Indian would possess."[6]

21

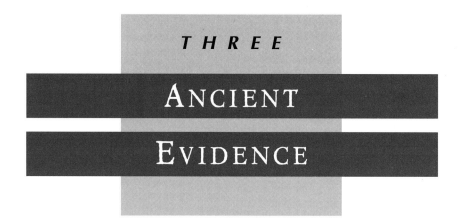

THREE

ANCIENT

EVIDENCE

Back at Arequipa, Juanita's team proceeded with their investigation. Her team of scientists had little experience with frozen bodies, so they consulted experts on other mummies. Some of the experts were ones who studied the few Inca mummies previously recovered from mountaintops. Unfortunately, since archaeologists rarely find frozen bodies, experts couldn't offer scientists all the information they needed. They had to create their own ways to investigate the ice maiden's body.

Once out of nature's high-altitude freezer, there was danger that Juanita's body could defrost and damage historic and scientific evidence. The team knew they had to find the perfect temperature at which to keep her. They suspected that keeping her body and clothing at a different temperature than her dried-out head would be the best way to preserve the girl. It proved to be an impossible task. They didn't want to remove the young girl's head, but they couldn't afford to have a special freezer case built. In the end, they decided to store her at the proper temperature for her body and clothing.

The team consulted the Ice Man scientists, who advised them that removing Juanita's clothing should be their first priority. From their experience with Ice Man, they knew it could help to save both the clothing and the girl's body. Even so, the task proved to be a real challenge. In her grave, snow melted and froze again in the young girl's clothing. If the team tried to remove the clothing while it was still frozen, they risked ripping it. If they let the clothing sit at room temperature, then Juanita's body might defrost too much.[1]

A Slow Process

To solve their dilemma, the team—with help from textile expert Bill Conklin—got together for a brainstorming session. Brainstorming happens when a group of people share ideas about how to solve a problem. Using their combined knowledge of chemistry and physics, the scientists discussed and considered many solutions to their problem. They knew they would have to defrost the ice-laden cloth and absorb the melted water at the same time.

They decided that small pieces of white cotton towel could do both jobs. Heated with a blow-dryer and laid on the mummy's clothing, pieces of towel would not only melt the ice but would absorb the meltwater, too. If they kept ice packs on Juanita's skin, her body could stay out of the freezer for more than a half hour at a time. For days, the scientists heated the small squares of cloth and laid them on her clothing. As the cloth defrosted, they slowly and painstakingly peeled it off her body.

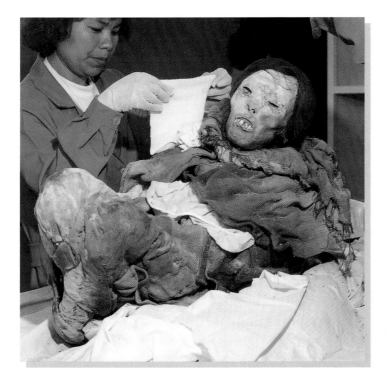

Scientists used small, heated pieces of cloth to defrost the frozen Juanita without harming the mummy's delicate body and clothing.

Occasionally, clumps of ice hidden within Juanita's clothing slowed the scientists' progress. Heated towels just couldn't melt these tiny lakes of ice, so the scientists again put their inventive thinking to the test. In the end, they decided to inject hot sterile water into the clumps with a hypodermic needle, all the while keeping the ice surrounded by white towels.[2]

INCA FASHION SENSE

As they untangled Juanita's clothing, Conklin and the team became more excited by what they found. Beneath her rough outer wrappings, they discovered her *lliclla,* a beautifully woven garment she wore around her shoulders as a shawl. A silver *tupu,* or shawl pin, held the cloth together in the front. Tupus were common items in an Inca woman's wardrobe. To historians, the presence of shawl pins on an Inca skeleton or body usually indicates a woman.

We know from historical accounts that the Inca women were very fashionable. In 1553 Spanish historian Pedro de Cieza de Leon wrote that the dress of the ladies of Cuzco (formerly the Inca capital) was "the most graceful and rich that has been seen up to this time in all the Indies." All Inca women wove cloth, from the lowliest peasants to the highest Inca royalty. Only a few examples of that cloth remain. From these, textile experts always believed the weavers never varied much from the traditional Inca geometric patterns and colors. Until, that is, they removed the lliclla to reveal Juanita's *aksu.*

An aksu was a dress worn by all Inca women. Like her lliclla, Juanita's aksu was a simple square of cloth. She wrapped it around her body and fastened it with tupus. Although Juanita's shawl echoes the same patterns and colors found on Inca clothing displayed in museums, her aksu is quite different. Whoever wove Juanita's aksu introduced a new color concept, banding the buttery yellow dress in broad strokes of plum and red. To the experts, it showed that at least some Inca didn't always dress in the traditional manner. The lliclla and aksu are so different it is almost as if the ice maiden echoes the modern teenage clothing style of wearing a plaid flannel shirt over a tie-dyed T-shirt. Scientists hope to some day remove Juanita's aksu. Right now, it's pinned beneath her arms, and she grips the edge of it tightly in her right hand.

The artifacts buried with Juanita are dressed identically to her. The statues and clothing were made in Cuzco. Similar examples turn up throughout the former Inca empire, a fact that indicates how widespread the traditions were.

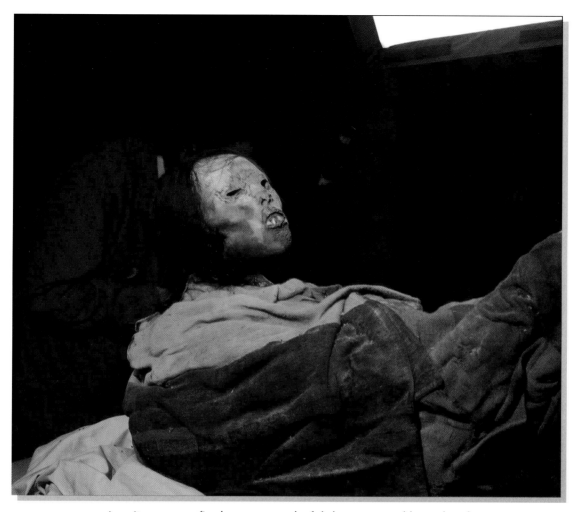

Juanita wears a finely woven, colorful dress covered by a shawl.

As they removed her wrappings, the scientists discovered a black alpaca thread woven into the girl's pigtail. The other end had been tied to her *chumpi,* or belt. They also discovered tiny carvings of two drinking vessels, a box, and a doglike animal that dangled by woolen threads from her tupu. Scientists have not yet figured out the significance of these carvings and the black alpaca thread.[3]

JUANITA REVISITED

There are few examples of how Inca women actually wore their brightly colored squares of cloth. Juanita presented the textile experts a perfect opportunity to learn more. To get a clear picture of what Juanita's costume looked like, Bill Conklin went to a Peruvian market and bought yards of plain, white cloth. He then cut it into squares the same size as Juanita's lliclla and aksu. Next, he found a twelve-year-old Peruvian girl, just Juanita's size. Conklin dressed her in the outfit, using a tupu to hold the shawl together. It was almost as if Juanita had come to life. The cloth, though not woven with colors like the ice maiden's clothing, helped the textile expert see how the fabric draped over the girl's body. An artist for *National Geographic* took pictures so later he would be able to draw her outfit accurately.

Back in the United States, Conklin used a computer to duplicate the design on Juanita's clothing. The artist used the photos he took and Conklin's computer-generated patterns to paint a picture of what Juanita may have looked like before she met her fate on the mountaintop. Her young female companion wore a feathered headdress, so the artist depicted Juanita with one, even though none was found with the ice maiden.[4]

LIFE AND DEATH

And what of the girl beneath the clothing? Her long black hair falls down her back in a braid. She has a thin, graceful neck and well-muscled arms. Despite her climb to a high mountaintop, where she knew she would die, she wears a pleasant expression. It was brought on, perhaps, by drinking corn beer, called *chicha*. Like other Inca sacrificial victims, the Inca spiritual leaders likely gave her this beer and perhaps other drugs to ease her symptoms of altitude sickness and the fear of death.[5]

To understand more about Juanita, the scientists sent her to the United States for further testing. In May 1996 she flew on an airplane in a specially designed freezer case donated by an American corporation. At Johns Hopkins University in Maryland, scientists used needles in a procedure called a needle biopsy to take tissue samples from Juanita's stomach, knees, and other parts of her body.

The sample taken from her knees shows Juanita's bones were normal and healthy for a girl her age, about fourteen years old. By analyzing the samples taken from her stomach, scien-

It is difficult to protect high-altitude archaeological sites from looting and destruction. By sending Juanita out of Peru for study, scientists can use the latest methods to learn about her and the artifacts. To respect the beliefs and concerns of the native peoples, archaeologists carefully excavated and conserved the site. Juanita will eventually be returned to a museum in Arequipa.

The carefully wrapped ice maiden enters a computed tomography (CT) scanning machine. The CT scanner provided many cross-section X rays, which were combined by computer to let scientists see inside the body from different angles.

tists discovered the remains of a vegetarian meal eaten within six to eight hours before she died. Scientists continue to analyze her stomach contents to determine exactly the type of food she ate and how soon before her death she ate it.

The scientists put Juanita through a computed tomography (CT) machine. This state-of-the-art scanner took 691 thin cross-section X rays of Juanita's body. Aided by a computer the machine turned the X rays into video images, which allowed scientists to manipulate the view of the young time traveler and to see her from many angles without moving her.

Historians know the Inca sometimes left their sacrificial victims alive on the mountain, where they died of exposure to the cold and wind. Others were strangled or hit on the head. Using the CT scans, scientists discovered that Juanita died from a heavy blow to the area above her right temple. It left a fracture in her skull two inches long and caused her brain to bleed from the injury. The internal wound produced so much blood that it pushed her brain to one side.

Hitting Juanita on the head seems like a cruel, horrible thing to do, but it may have been the best thing for her. Johan Reinhard believes her killers were kind and cushioned the blow with a folded blanket. This way, Juanita never regained consciousness. We can take some comfort in knowing that she believed she was an honored victim, a messenger from her people to their powerful gods.[6]

FOUR

SUN GODS AND SACRIFICE

His name was Viracocha, and to the ancient people of Peru, he was the sun—a god in their eyes. From the time she was a small girl, Juanita heard many of the stories her people told of this brilliant deity. In one, Viracocha takes pity on humans when he looks earthward and sees them living like wild animals. He sends his son and daughter, Manco Capac and Mama Ocllo, to earth, instructing them to teach the people how to build villages and raise crops. He also gives the pair a staff of solid gold two fingers thick and tells them to probe the soil with it till they find a place where it sinks deep into the earth with a single thrust. It is here, he tells them, that they must build a city.

According to the legend, as Manco Capac and Mama Ocllo wander the land, their sun–father passes daily to watch their progress. After a time, Manco Capac and Mama Ocllo come upon a fertile valley. On a sun-soaked morning, Manco Capac appears as a shining god himself, cloaked in a mantle studded with gold disks. He hurls the golden staff miles into the valley, where it buries itself deep in the soil.

It is then that Manco Capac declares himself son of the sun, an Inca. He and his sister take the land from the native people and build a city. They name it Cuzco, navel of the world. Over the course of Inca reign, it would become the most magnificent metropolis in South America.[1]

29

While Juanita's people told stories to explain their creation, archaeologists have a different explanation. Historical evidence shows the Inca emperor Manco Capac was a real person. He rose to power in A.D. 1200 from a South American Indian people who spoke a language called Quechua. Today when we refer to the Inca, we mean all the people of the Inca empire, but originally, only the emperor could bear the royal title of Inca.

There were thirteen Inca emperors in all before the Spanish conquest in 1532, among them Pachachuti ("He Who Restores the Earth"), Yahuar Huaccac ("He Who Weeps Blood"), and Lloque Yupanqui ("Unforgettable Left-handed One"). In less than a century, each one did his part to unite various tribes and to expand the empire 2,500 miles, from modern-day Colombia in the north to central Chile in the south.

This in itself was an amazing feat. The western coast of South America is home to the Andes mountains, second only in height and ruggedness to the Himalayas, on the border of India and Tibet. In their conquest, the Inca surmounted ice-encrusted mountains 20,000 feet high. Their expansion halted only temporarily when they encountered mile-deep canyons gouged into the highlands by a roaring river. In the south, expanses of desert slowed but did not turn back their progress.

And there were other obstacles. Not all the tribes inhabiting the length of the continent were Quechua, so the Inca had to conquer them. Since not everyone wished to be conquered, the clever Inca devised ways to convince the various tribes that conquest was for the best. Sometimes they kidnapped a tribe's religious idols and held them captive in Cuzco. Or they took the children of conquered nobility to Cuzco to educate them. The tribes could do little once that happened, or they would risk losing the things they loved most. To soften the blow, the Inca frequently adopted some of the conquered tribe's religious beliefs as their own, and they invited their chiefs to Cuzco, where they feted them with celebrations and tributes.

The Inca also incorporated the conquered

The Inca culture depended heavily on the llama, an animal related to the camel and native to South America. The people used its wool for clothing and its meat for food. As a beast of burden, a llama could carry 80 pounds. Llamas were also used for sacrifices. Today, llamas are still an important animal to the descendants of the Inca.

*An early depiction
of some Inca nobles,
published in May 1752*

31

tribe's arts and science into their own culture, and strengthened their own as they did. From the brass-smelting Collas of Bolivia, the Inca learned to fashion brass tools and utensils. From the Aimaras, they learned to make beautiful gold jewelry and surgical tools to perform trepanning, a primitive brain operation. To further cement the bond, the Inca emperor sent his people to the newly conquered tribes to teach them the arts, crafts, and language of their new rulers. By 1470, around the time Juanita died, the Inca had defeated the last of their enemies. By 1532, the empire's population numbered 12 million.[2]

HIGH-TECH SOCIETY

The Inca used communication, transportation, and a strictly governed society to keep the empire together. When they encountered deep ravines, they spanned them with suspension bridges made of a strong fiber from the agave plant. They built more than 14,000 miles of elaborate roadways to transact the empire's business. In the uplands, where drifting snow was a problem, they edged these roads with stone walls to keep the snow away. They built adobe walls along desert roads to shelter them from drifting sand.

According to the Spanish chronicler Pedro de Cieza de Leon, Inca roads were the greatest in the world, "laid through deep valleys and over high mountains, through snow-banks and quagmires, through live rock and along raging rivers; in some places smooth and paved, in others tunneled through cliffs, skirting gorges, linking snowpeaks with stairways and rest stops: everywhere clean-swept and litter-free, with lodgings, storehouses, and temples of the sun."

The empire's news moved along these roads, transported by thousands of *chasquis,* or post-runners, who lived in roadside shacks during their fifteen-day shift. On the job, the men waited to hear the call of a conch shell, which meant a fellow chasquis was approaching with a message to pass along. Each chasquis knew a 2-mile stretch of road well enough to run during any kind of weather, day or night. The messages and other business traveled 150 to 200 miles a day.[3] This system of rapid communication helped to unify the empire.

FOOD FOR EVERYONE

The Inca elevated agriculture to high art. The people became experts at growing crops on the most inhospitable landscape. On steep slopes, they constructed row after row of stone walls, fifteen feet high. Between these walls, they placed dirt and

A gold figure pendant (above)
and tiny gold figure (right)
show the skill of Inca artists.

The Inca were skilled at building roads (left) *and suspension bridges* (right).

leveled it off enough to plant crops. Inca descendants still use these terraces that look like giant stairs cut into the mountainside. The Inca irrigated vast stretches of desert with elaborately constructed irrigation systems. They grew squash, sweet potatoes, cotton, yams, herbs, beans, chiles, coca, and a type of grain called *quinoa.* They turned *sara,* or corn, into breads, cakes, and chicha. One of their staples was *chuño,* which is frozen dehydrated potatoes.

Most commoners farmed, and it was their job to provide food for the empire. The head of each family received from the government a tupú, a plot of land large enough to plant 100 pounds of corn. In turn, each son received a tupú, while daughters received half a tupú. The Inca decreed that one-third of the harvest from common lands be given to the emperor and his family, priests, and other officials. Another third went to soldiers, orphans, the elderly, and sick. The rest went to the community. Administrators, called *chunca camayoc,* managed groups of ten farmers. A *pachaca chunca camayoc* managed ten of these groups. Another manager oversaw fifty groups, and so on up to the *hunu camayoc,* the chief of ten

*In order to grow crops on steep slopes, the Inca developed a way of
terracing still used today. In this photo, Inca ruins can be seen above the terraces.*

thousand, one of the Big Ears. The noble Big Ears got their name from the large gold disks they wore in their earlobes.[4]

DIVINE ORDER

All this was impossible without a well-ordered society. To better control their subjects, the Inca divided them into groups. An administrator headed up each one. Males and females formed ten groups, based on age. Men from fifteen to twenty years old became warriors. Warriors' wives spun wool, wove cloth, and fashioned clothing. After a turn at being a warrior, the men often became servants to nobility. Older women cared for the children.

The youngest, up to five years old, could stay with their parents. After that, boys became top-spinners until they were nine years old, trained in the Inca way and punished for bad behavior. Boys from nine to twelve protected the harvest, while older boys tended herds and hunted animals and birds. Younger girls learned to cook, spin wool, and prepare chicha. Young women from twelve to thirty years old became wives. In return for their hard work, the government provided everything the people needed.

The Inca leaders kept their subjects under control by punishment as well as by order. Lesser criminals received anything from merely public rebuke to exile, usually to a coca plantation. The worst were stoned to death, hanged by their feet until dead, or thrown from a cliff. Sometimes the Inca administered a punishment called *hiwaya*, the dropping of a big rock on a man's back. Despite how rigid it may seem, the system worked surprisingly well, and for a time, most people lived happy, prosperous lives.[5]

SON OF THE SUN

The Inca emperor, divine ruler of the universe, oversaw these happy lives. Until chosen as a gift to the gods, Juanita may never have met her emperor. But the fact that all believed he descended from the sun itself would have been enough to evoke powerful feelings in the girl. Each Inca ruler claimed Manco Capac as an ancestor, and in so doing, claimed descent from the sun itself.

The son of the sun ruled from a solid gold throne, and surrounded himself with servants, courtiers, and nobility. He never wore the same clothes twice, instead giving once-worn outfits to his family and relatives. His servants fulfilled his every wish.[6]

When an Inca ruler died, the Big Ears chose the most capable of his sons to replace him. Instead of using his father's palace, the new Inca had one built, filling it with patios, gardens, hallways, and magnificent rooms. Gold and silver were so plentiful that thin sheets of it were used to cover walls in much the same way we use wallpaper.

Sometimes the Inca ruler journeyed outside of Cuzco to survey his kingdom. He brought his entourage of nobles and servants, who carried him on an elaborately decorated litter. As the procession passed through each town, the people scattered flowers in the path of their beloved emperor-god. Some loved the Inca ruler so much that when he died, the most grief-stricken followers committed suicide by stuffing leaves in their mouths and suffocating.[7]

FIVE

MOUNTAIN GODS
AND MUMMIES

Divine rule centered on the city of Cuzco, which the Inca people believed was the center of the universe. All around Cuzco stood the symbols that honored the sun gods—fountains and altars, life-sized birds, reptiles, amphibians, and human figures made of gold. In the botanical gardens of Cuzco, artisans sculpted in gold every plant and animal that lived within the empire. In the city's temples, old women wearing golden masks fanned flies away from the mummies of their dead emperors.

Priests served the gods and Inca, too. They adhered to strict rules, eating no meat and drinking only water. Macaw feathers, jewels, gold, and vicuna skulls adorned their tunics. In the Sun Temple, priests sacrificed llamas and read their internal organs for signs of the future. They made offerings of chicha, maize, coca, birds, lizards, and frogs, among other things.

A huge golden disk embossed with a human face presided over the ceremonies, as well as Punchao, a gold statue that represented the sun child. Inside Punchao stood a golden chalice containing the dried hearts of previous Inca rulers. Sometimes Napa, the white llama, attended the ceremonies. Napa wore a red shirt and tassles of wool at the tips of its ears. It offered chicha to the gods by kicking over crocks of potent brew.[1]

Priests also served at the religious festivities that abounded in cities and towns during every month of the year. The largest one, Inti Raimi, the winter sun festi-

The sons of nobles attended a huge five-block school where they learned religion, history, language, and how to read *quipu*. Quipu are knotted strings that recorded the statistics and history of the empire.

val, occurred on the first day of their solar year in June. Like the many other festivals, Inti Raimi beat with the pulse of trumpets, shell horns, drums, and rattles. Nobility from the far-flung provinces descended on Cuzco. Some wore animal skins and capes made of bright bird feathers. Many of the mountain chiefs wore costumes made from the outstretched wings of the condor, which they considered sacred. At dawn on the first day of Inti Raimi, the Inca and his nobles traveled to Joy plaza, the holiest of plazas in the realm. There, they laid on their backs with their faces toward the east, ready to kiss the sun's rays as they overtook the plaza.

Celebrations and festivities of all kinds marked Inca life. Some celebrations honored the gods that blessed the crops. As they still do today, the people trooped to the river, carrying the mummies of their ancestors, where they washed them

Modern Peruvians still enjoy a number of ancient Inca celebrations. The Inti Raimi festival is one of the largest.

and applied a fresh coat of corn gruel to their skin. Afterward, they put on their finest clothing and danced with the mummies in the plaza.[2]

THE GODS ARE EVERYWHERE

The explanation for Juanita's high-mountain death comes from these strong spiritual beliefs. The Inca found their own meanings for what happened in the natural world. They believed that many gods ruled their world. Every day Inti, which is another name for their sun god, traveled across the sky. At night he swam below the earth until it was time to rise again. They called Inti's wife Mama Quilla (Kilya); she was the moon and queen of the sky. They explained thunder by saying it came from their god Ilyapa, who carried a club and slung thunderbolts to earth.

The Inca called their ancient corn goddess Sora Mama, and Llama Mama protected the llama herds. When Pacha Kuyuchik tossed in his sleep, he caused the earth to rumble, in what we call an earthquake. They explained lunar eclipses as a celestial puma trying to devour the moon. To scare it away, they shouted, banged on drums, blew trumpets, and shot arrows at the sky.[3]

MYSTERIOUS MOUNTAIN GODS

These gods were part of everyday Inca life, but there was one set of gods that stood out among the others. These were the mountain deities that dominated the Inca landscape and imagination. The mountains weren't just representative of the gods—they were the gods themselves.

The mountains affected weather, trapping rain clouds on their far side or letting them pass over their high summits. Volcanoes spewed ash, which clogged water systems and covered crops. Ash melted snow on mountaintops, which in turn affected the amount of water coming down from upper elevations. The mountain gods could kill with an avalanche or rock fall, lightning, or a blizzard.[4]

To the Inca, the mountains were spiritual landmarks that held magical powers. Stories and legends sprung up about each. For example, the mountain Tata Sabaya's notch at its summit came from having a tooth knocked out during a fight with Sajama, the highest peak in Bolivia. Diviners and soothsayers, who usually foretold the future by looking at llama intestines, spider legs, and corn kernels, often called on the mountain spirits to assist them in their predictions. Sometimes the mountain gods appeared to them in dreams. Even today, Inca de-

The Inca believed the mountains were sacred. They often built a sacrificial altar honoring mountain gods at the very summit of a mountain, as they did here at a height of 18,600 feet.

scendants believe that mountain gods, or *apus*, can take any form and frequently wander the mountain passes.[5]

CAPACOCHA

It is no surprise then that the Inca would want to please these powerful mountain gods. To honor them, the Inca developed an intricate offering ceremony called Capacocha. Not much is known about this ancient ritual. What little we do know we have learned from the Spanish conquistadors who took time to write about it.

Capacocha was not an everyday ceremony. They celebrated it only during im-

41

portant events, such as the death of an Inca emperor. They also performed the Capacocha ritual during disastrous events, such as drought, disease, epidemic, earthquake, or continued bad weather.[6]

> People carried personal charms—*huacas*, or idols—which they called brother or sister or other endearing names.

> During the moon festival, held to ward off sickness and disease, all dogs, deformed people, and visitors had to leave the city.

To please their gods, the Inca believed they had to travel to the very tops of the mountains, a rigorous, difficult climb in the thin, frigid air of high altitude. At the mountaintop, they offered the mountain gods the very best they had. Sometimes that meant food, drink, or golden statues of llamas and figurines. Frequently it meant children—from five years old to twenty years old.

But the offerings weren't just *any* children. Those sacrificed to the mountain were usually the sons and daughters of high-ranking nobles or village chiefs. To be chosen, the children had to be physically perfect, with no blemishes or handicaps that marred their appearance. By offering their very best, the Inca hoped to stop disaster in its tracks.

While it may seem strange to think about killing a child for a god, the children's families felt honored by the choice. Sometimes they were first to offer their child for sacrifice. To them, it brought honor to the family and linked them forever with Viracocha, ancestor of their Inca emperor. Not only that, but once the child died, he or she was thought to also become a god.

Capacocha began with the child, either a boy or a girl, and the family traveling to Cuzco. There they would meet the emperor and participate in huge feasts in the child's honor. Capacocha was a time of great celebration. It was so great, in fact, that one Spanish historian said that when one victim passed through her village on her way to be sacrificed, she told her neighbors: "You can finish with me now because I could not be more honored than by the feasts which they celebrated for me in Cuzco."[7]

MORE MUMMIES

Juanita is not the only sacrificial victim discovered on a mountaintop. Climbers found the first Capacocha victim ever discovered on a high peak in Chile in 1954.

The boy was about eight or nine years old when he climbed the mountain El Plomo. After he died, freezing temperatures preserved his little body. Five hundred years later, he still wears red face paint with four yellow lines radiating from his nose and upper lips to his cheeks. Before he died, someone oiled and plaited his hair into more than 200 braids.

They adorned his body with a silver pendant and a wide silver bracelet. He still wears a sleeveless tunic and moccasins made of llama wool. Investigators also discovered five cloth pouches with the young boy. These pouches contain snips of his hair, baby teeth, fingernail clippings, and red threads that had been saved by his family to be buried with him. It meant that in the afterlife, his spirit wouldn't have to go looking for these missing pieces of his body.

Ceremonies to appease mountain gods often included the sacrifice of a young child or children. This mummy of a young boy was found on a high peak in Chile in 1954.

When scientists investigated the body, they discovered that the fingers of the boy's left hand had turned white. They interpret this to mean that he likely suffered frostbite on the mountaintop. His feet and ankles were swollen, too, as if he had walked for a long while over rough terrain. He has type O blood, typical of Indians in South America.

Archaeologists know the Inca often gave their sacrificial victims chicha, perhaps to ease the pain of a high-altitude climb and to help them face death. Studies of the boy's liver were inconclusive for alcohol, but vomit stains on his tunic suggest he may have been drunk. The El Plomo corpse also yielded a virus that causes warts. Until they discovered the virus, scientists were never sure it existed in the Western Hemisphere before Europeans arrived—finding the virus in the El Plomo corpse meant it did.[8]

Archaeologists also continue to study another sacrificial victim, a boy found on Mount Aconcagua. His body had been wrapped in several blankets made of vicuna wool and cotton, decorated with bird and geometric designs. He wears an Andean tunic, woven sandals, an outer cape of yellow feathers, and a necklace of multicolored beads.[9] His skin was coated with a red pigment. His sacrificers buried his body within a semicircle of stones. Like many Capacocha victims, he is in a sitting position with his arms wrapped around his legs.

SIX
LAST
DAYS

It is bright morning, and Juanita awakens. Joy and dread filled the night, keeping sleep away until its very last, dark hours. Outside her window, she hears the noise of people preparing for her festival: clanging bells, shouting, footsteps, and the low rumble of something shifting across the courtyard. Today, hundreds of people will celebrate her last days of life as a mortal girl. It will be her first time meeting the Inca, and she wonders what he will be like. Proud and regal, yes, and perhaps kind as well. She knows her family is proud of her. She could see it in their faces as they entered Cuzco yesterday. They are humbled, too, by what awaits.

Later, during the festival, as dancers whirl, she sees the sadness her mother tries to hide. Perhaps Juanita looks toward Mount Ampato and wonders about her journey to its faraway summit. She may have heard things about other children being chosen for this honor. She looks again at her family and the mass of people gathered here in Cuzco. How fearsome and wondrous to know you will soon meet your gods.

The next day, her procession winds its way out of Cuzco, heading toward the mountain. Llamas sway beneath their loads. The priests march ahead. Villagers follow. Children clap their hands as she passes, and young boys race beside the festive parade. Juanita's memories race, too, back to the previous days' festivities, to the Inca and his magnificent golden robes, to the solemn way he said good-bye. Then memory takes her further back to her village and to the warmth of friends and family. It is hard to think about life with the gods when you have felt so much love on earth.

In no time at all, she sees the mountain looming before her. The people who follow grow

45

more lively as they approach. Once they begin the climb, some of them drop away, though many will continue on to the base camp at 16,000 feet. Here, they rest for the night. The young girl watches sleepily as others unload bundles from the llamas' backs. This night, the animals stand in their stone corral, bright eyes blinking in the dark. Juanita sleeps within a walled enclosure. Ichu insulates the floor and colorful blankets keep out most of the wind. She is tired from the climb but sleeps fitfully.

At daybreak, the priests' helpers load the llamas with the bundles of pottery, food, and chicha they will offer at the mountaintop. As they ascend, Juanita weakens. The air is bone-chilling cold, and she cannot breathe well. It scares her that the gods can take away her breath like this. She is now so weak the priests must carry her up the mountain to the camp at 19,200 feet where they spend the night. They awaken the next morning to make offerings of food and drink. The priests carry Juanita another 1,200 feet to the shoulder of the summit covered with ichu, and all sleep another night before climbing to the sacrificial platform at the crater's rim.

A modern herd of llamas passes centuries-old walls built by the Inca, who used llamas as pack animals and for their wool. People of the Andes use llamas today in much the same way.

She has never seen the world from this height—it is an awesome sight. The land stretches below her in folds and ridges of gray and green. Up here, she can almost touch the clouds. Juanita tries to imagine the people returning to work in Cuzco and the family and friends she leaves behind. But she is tired now. At the crater's rim, near the sacrificial platform, Juanita shivers in her blanket while the attendants complete their final preparations. Finally, one of the priests gathers her in his arms and places her in the center of the platform. As they call out to their gods, Juanita can barely think. A drink of chicha, given earlier by a priest, has quelled her fear and nausea. Juanita's mind stops struggling to understand the intermingled dreams of her gods and parents. Meanwhile, one of the priests folds a blanket. He places it over her before another delivers the crushing blow to her head. Later, they will return to fill her grave with earth brought from below.[1]

SINISTER FORCES

Of course, we cannot know if Juanita's last days went exactly like this. But by studying historical accounts, the artifacts, and bodies discovered on mountaintops, we can piece together a picture of what her final days may have been like. We do know that Juanita probably died not knowing life would soon change for her people.

In 1532, a sinister force in the form of Spanish conquistadors raided the land of the Inca. Armed with only 168 men and 37 horses, Francisco Pizarro, named by the king of Spain as governor of Peru, began to systematically demolish the empire. It seems odd that so few men could conquer a strong nation, but an earlier Inca civil war helped their cause. Along the way, Spanish conquistadors found allies in natives unhappy with the reign of the Inca. These Indians proved to be more than willing to help overthrow the Inca government.

Pizarro's men pillaged the Inca temples and storehouses. Spanish bookkeepers busily itemized the loot. By the end of 1533, accounts show the Spaniards had acquired over 24 tons of treasure: idols and chalices, jewelry, altars, and fountains. They melted down all the gold they could find and paid it out in shares to the soldiers and others. They sent the rest of the bounty to King Charles of Spain. It turned out to be the richest treasure ever taken by a king.

> The Inca did not understand that gold would buy things. They thought the Spaniards ate it.

More Spaniards arrived, spurred on by their desire for gold. The Spanish set up their government, abandoning Cuzco in favor of a capital in Lima, Peru. They had

An artist's interpretation of Pizarro taking the Inca emperor prisoner

effectively conquered an empire, one that had seemed destined for greater things. They subjected the people, took their land, and forced them to work on large farms, called haciendas. The natives weren't immune to new diseases the Spanish brought, and many died.[2]

Despite all this, the Inca traditions survived, though the lives of the Indians practicing them have not been the same since conquest. The official language of the government is Spanish, but most people living in the highlands of Peru still speak Quechua. They practice the Christianity the Spaniards brought with them, but it is Christianity enriched by their ancient Inca traditions. Healers, called *curanderos,* still predict the future by reading the entrails, or intestines, of animals. Families still make offerings, too. In the markets, merchants sell *despachos,* small offering bundles filled with cookies, small statues, seashells, incense, llama fat, and coca leaves.

The highlands Indians continue to honor their mountains—many still regard them as direct ancestors and call them "father." In modern-day pilgrimages to the mountain, an *ukuku,* or bear man, retrieves ice from a glacier and melts it. Villagers use the meltwater for healing. Foreign climbers honor the mountain, too. Johan Reinhard and his colleagues always make offerings before ascending the mountain.[3]

*A modern highland Indian couple travel an ancient
Inca roadway high in the mountains they revere.*

Juanita would never know that 500 years after her death, two men would happen upon her frozen body. And she wouldn't know that less than a year after Reinhard discovered her body he would find another girl on Sara Sara, a mountain the Indians still consider one of the most sacred.

In 1983, on a previous expedition to Sara Sara's summit, Johan Reinhard found a silver tupu. Since it's unlikely that Inca women would have climbed a mountain without some purpose, he knew he might find a woman's body on the summit. A return expedition in the fall of 1996 proved him right. First, one of his team members discovered a small cloth bag with coca leaves, a traditional mountain offering. As they excavated further, they found a small, silver female figure and the top of a skull protruding from the frozen ground. Though Juanita is better preserved than Sarita, they hope the young girl's body will contribute more to their understanding of the Inca.[4]

In the 500 years since Juanita's death, the world has undergone enormous changes. Where her people once climbed the highest peaks wearing only sandals, woolen socks, and thickly woven clothing, modern climbers use high-tech materials and climbing gear. The Inca communicated with their gods from the mountains through ritual and sacrifice. Expeditions today use modern technology to communicate in a much more complicated world.[5]

Writers and photographers for Public Television's *Nova* accompanied the archaeological team to the summit of Sara Sara. Using a laptop computer, they submitted up-to-date stories and digital photographs by uplinking them to a communications satellite. *Nova* then downloaded the reports and images and put them on the World Wide Web, where thousands of people kept tabs on the team's progress.[6]

It's not often we have a chance to see history in this way. As long as we continue to discover messengers from the past such as Juanita, we will continue to learn more about the life of the Inca and other ancient cultures.

T I M E L I N E

MUMMIES OF
THE INCA

AROUND A.D. 1200   Manco Capac rises to power as the first Inca.

AROUND A.D. 1495   Juanita sacrificed on Mount Ampato

A.D.1532   Francisco Pizzaro finally succeeds in conquering the Inca after two previously unsuccessful attempts in 1524 and 1526.

BY 1533   Spaniards acquire over twenty-four tons of Inca treasure.

1954   young boy mummy, about eight or nine years old, discovered at the summit of El Plomo in Chile

1983   Johan Reinhard first visits the sacred mountain Sara Sara.

1985   young boy mummy, about seven years old, discovered at the summit of Mount Aconcagua in Argentina

1993   Miguel Zárate's brother climbs Mount Ampato and returns to report the summit covered with a thick layer of ice and snow.

SEPT. 1995   Johan Reinhard and Miguel Zárate climb Mount Ampato and find most of the snow and ice on Ampato have melted. They also discover the mummified corpse of Juanita.

OCT. 1995   Johan Reinhard returns to Mount Ampato with an eighteen-member archaeological team where they discover the remains of two more sacrificed children.

SEPT. 1996   Thirteen years after he first climbs the sacred mountain Sara Sara, Johan Reinhard returns with an archaeological team and a team from Public Broadcasting Station's program *Nova*. At the top, the team discovers a mummified girl. Though she's not as well preserved as Juanita, scientists hope Sarita will help them learn more about the ancient Inca.

1995–PRESENT   Scientists continue to conduct scientific studies on Juanita's body.

GLOSSARY

adobe   sun-dried brick made of a yellow silt or clay deposited by rivers

aksu   a piece of cloth worn as a dress by Inca women

allies   people united for a common cause

alpaca   a relative of the llama with long, silky hair that can be woven into fabric

apus   mountain gods

archaeologist   a person who gathers knowledge about historic or prehistoric cultures

artifact   any object made or changed by humans

Big Ears   Inca noblemen, noted for the large gold disks they wore in their earlobes

brainstorming   unrestrained idea-generating (usually done by a group)

Capacocha   a sacrificial ceremony that involved killing a boy or a girl as an offering to the gods

chalice   a drinking cup

chasquis   postrunners for the Inca who moved mail and messages through the Inca empire

chicha   corn beer

chronicler   a person who records the events of history

chumpi   Juanita's belt

chuño   dried frozen potatoes used as food by ancient Inca as well as their descendants

conquistador   Spanish explorers who conquered South America during the sixteenth century

courtier   a person in attendance at a royal court

CT scan   computed tomography; a computer-generated X-ray process that shows the internal structure of the human body

curanderos   healers

dehydration   a lack of water in the body

deity   a god or goddess

despachos   offering bundles that may contain candy, coca leaves, candles, statuettes, etc.

DNA   deoxyribonucleic acid; a complex molecule found in human cells by which familial characteristics are passed from parent to child

entourage   a group of personal attendants

entrails   intestines

exile   to be separated from one's home or country, usually forcibly

expedition   a journey made for a specific purpose

fardo   a mummy bundle

gorge   a small canyon

hacienda   a large Spanish farm in the Americas

hiwaya   a punishment in which a large rock was dropped on a man's back

huacas   personal idols

hypoxia   a lack of oxygen to the tissues of the body

ichu   wild grass

Inti Raimi   winter sun festival

irrigation system   a way of bringing water to crop plants

litter   a vehicle carried by humans; consists of a couch and platform suspended between two poles

llama   an animal related to a camel; used in the Andes as a beast of burden and a source of wool

lliclla   Juanita's shawl

Mama Quilla   moon goddess of the Inca

Manco Capac   son of the sun god Viracocha and founder of the Inca people

metropolis   city

Napa   a sacred white llama dressed in a red shirt with red tassels at the tips of its ears

needle biopsy   taking samples of bone and tissues with a needle

neolithic   final stage of the Stone Age

pillage   violent robbery, especially during wartime

pinnacles   a pointed formation

Francisco Pizarro   led the Spanish conquest of the Inca

plaited   braided

Punchao   sun child of the Inca

quagmire   boggy ground

Quechua   the language spoken by descendants of the ancient Inca

quinoa   a grain grown and eaten by the Inca and their descendants

quipu   knotted strings by which the Inca emperor and his people kept business records and other information

ravine   a narrow, steep-sided valley

ritual   a way people formally honor or celebrate something, usually repeated regularly

sacrifice   offering animals, plants, objects, or humans to a god or goddess

shroud   something that covers or conceals, such as a piece of cloth

spondylus   shell of a sea mollusk

trepanning   a primitive brain operation performed by removing a piece of the skull

tunic   an outer garment with or without sleeves

tupu   a shawl pin

tupú   a plot of land

ukuku   a bear man who conducts religious ceremonies in the Andes

vicuna   a small relative of the llama whose fur is woven into cloth

Viracocha   sun god

SOURCE NOTES

ONE: MOUNTAIN DISCOVERY

1. S. Clark, B. Moffett, J. Peters, (producers/writers), "Ice Treasures of the Inca," *National Geographic Society,* Washington, D.C. (1996).

http://www.nationalgeographic.com/modules/mummy/index.html

Johan Reinhard, "Peru's Ice Maidens," *National Geographic* (June 1996): 62–81.

2. Ibid.

3. Ibid.

TWO: ARCHAEOLOGY AT ALTITUDE

1. David Roberts, "The Ice Man: Lone Traveler from the Copper Age," *National Geographic* (June 1993): 36–67.

2. Reinhard, "Peru's Ice Maidens," 62–81.

3. Ibid.

Liesl Clark, interview December 1996. Liesl Clark is an adventurer, writer, and online producer for *Nova Online: Ice Mummies of the Inca.*

Liesl Clark, (producer/writer), "Ice Mummies of the Inca." *Nova Online,* Boston, Mass., (1995/1996).

http://www.pbs.org:80/wgbh/pages/nova/peru/tabletext.html

Liesl Clark, (producer/writer), "Everest Quest," *Nova Online.* Boston, Mass.

http://www.pbs.org:80/wgbh/pages/nova/everest

4. Johan Reinhard, "High-Altitude Archaeology and Andean Mountain Gods," *The American Alpine Journal* (1983): 54–67; Reinhard, "Ice Maidens," 62–81.

5. Ibid.

6. Ibid.

THREE : ANCIENT EVIDENCE

1. Reinhard, "Ice Maidens," 62–81.

2. William Conklin, interview December 1996. Bill Conklin is an expert on pre-Colombian textiles, National Gallery of Art, Washington, D.C.

3. Ibid.; Reinhard, "Ice Maidens," 62–81.

4. Conklin, interview 1996.

5. Reinhard, "Ice Maidens," 62–81.

6. Johan Reinhard, "Mummies of Peru," *National Geographic* (January 1997): 36–43.

FOUR : SUN GODS AND SACRIFICE

1. Carleton Beals, *The Incredible Incas: Yesterday and Today* (Aylesbury, England: Abelard-Schuman Limited, 1973), 20–22; Loren McIntyre, *The Incredible Incas and Their Timeless Land* (Washington, D.C.: National Geographic Society, 1975), 36.

2. Ibid.

3. Beals, *Incredible Incas,* 128–130; McIntyre, *Incredible Incas and Timeless Land,* 22, 84; Clark, "Ice Mummies of the Inca," *Nova Online.*

4. Beals, *Incredible Incas,* 22, 26, 125–126; McIntyre, *Incredible Incas and Timeless Land,* 62–63.

5. Ibid.

6. Beals, *Incredible Incas,* 121.

7. Beals, *Incredible Incas,* 124.

FIVE : MOUNTAIN GODS AND MUMMIES

1. Beals, *Incredible Incas,* 25; McIntyre, *Incredible Incas and Timeless Land,* 61, 69

2. Beals, *Incredible Incas,* 145–147.

3. Ibid.; McIntyre.

4. Clark, "Ice Mummies of the Incas," *Nova Online;* Johan Reinhard, "Sacred Peaks of the Andes," *National Geographic* (March 1992): 84–111.

5. Ibid.

6. Clark, "Ice Mummies," *Nova Online.*

7. Ibid.; Reinhard, "Sacred Peaks," 84–111.

8. Thomas Besom, "Sacrifices of the High Andes," *Natural History* (April 1991): 66–68.

9. Juan Schobinger, "Sacrifices of the High Andes," *Natural History* (April 1991): 63–66.

SIX : LAST DAYS

1. Clark, "Ice Mummies," *Nova Online;* Reinhard, "Sacred Peaks," 84–111; Reinhard, "High Altitude," 54–67;

2. McIntyre, *Incredible Incas and Timeless Land,* 120–140; Clark, "Ice Mummies," *Nova Online.*

3. Reinhard, "Sacred Peaks," 84–111.

4. Clark, "Ice Mummies," *Nova Online.*

5. Reinhard, "High Altitude," 54–67.

6. Clark, "Ice Mummies," *Nova Online.*

FURTHER READING

Beals, Carleton. *The Incredible Incas: Yesterday and Today.* Aylesbury, England: Abelard-Schuman Limited, 1973.

Besom, Thomas. "Sacrifices of the High Andes." *Natural History* (April 1991): 66–68.

Clark, Liesl. Interview December 1996. Liesl Clark is an adventurer, writer, and online producer for *Nova Online:* "Ice Mummies of the Inca."

Clark, Liesl (producer/writer). "Ice Mummies of the Inca." *Nova Online.* Boston, Mass. (1995/1996).
http://www.pbs.org:80/wgbh/pages/nova/peru/tabletext.html

———. "Everest Quest." *Nova Online.* Boston, Mass.
http://www.pbs.org:80/wgbh/pages/nova/everest

Clark, S., B. Moffett, J. Peters. (producers/writers), "Ice Treasures of the Inca." National Geographic Society. Washington, D.C. (1996).
http://www.nationalgeographic.com/modules/mummy/index.html

McIntyre, Loren. *The Incredible Incas and Their Timeless Land.* Washington, D.C.: National Geographic Society, 1975.

Reinhard, Johan. "Peru's Ice Maidens." *National Geographic* (June 1996): 62–81.

———. "Mummies of Peru." *National Geographic* (January 1997): 36–43.

———. "Sacred Peaks of the Andes." *National Geographic* (March 1992): 84–111.

———. "High-Altitude Archaeology and Andean Mountain Gods." *The American Alpine Journal* (1983): 54–67.

Roberts, David. "The Ice Man: Lone Traveler from the Copper Age." *National Geographic* (June 1993): 36–67

Schobinger, Juan. "Sacrifices of the High Andes." *Natural History* (April 1991): 63–66.

INDEX

Aimaras, 32
aksu, 24, 26
Andes mountains, 10, 16, 30
archaeologists, 10, 16, 17, 19, 20, 22,
  26, 30, 44, 50
Arequipa, Peru, 13, 14, 22, 26
artifacts, 13, 14, 24, 26, 47

bacteria, 11
base camps, 18
Big Ears, 36, 37

Capacocha ritual, 41, 42, 44
Catholic University, 12, 14
celebrations and festivities, 30, 38, 39,
  41, 42, 45
Charles, King of Spain, 47
chasquis (post-runners), 32
chicha, 26, 34, 36, 38, 44, 46, 47
Christianity, 49
chunca camayoc, 34

chuño, 34
Collas, 32
computed tomography (CT) machine,
  28
condor, 39
Conklin, Bill, 23, 26
curanderos, 49
Cuzco, 24, 29, 30, 37–39, 42, 45, 47

de Betanzos, Juan, 21
de Leon, Pedro de Cieza, 24, 32
despachos, 49

El Plomo corpse, 43, 44

fardo. *See* mummy bundle
feathered headdresses, 8, 20, 26
figurines, 10, 19, 38, 42, 50. *See also*
  statuettes

grave sites, 19–21

haciendas, 48
high-altitude climbs, 16, 18, 26, 49
Himalaya Mountains, 16, 30
hiwaya, 36
huacas (idols), 42, 47
hunu camayoc, 34
hypoxia, 16, 17

Ice man, 14, 22
ichu, 19, 46
Inca empire, 8, 10, 14, 16, 18, 19, 21,
    30, 32, 34, 36, 38, 39, 47–50
  agriculture of the, 32, 34
  emperors of the, 30, 32, 34, 36–38,
    42
  females of the, 34, 36, 42
  gods of the, 10, 20, 28, 29, 37–42,
    44–46
  males of the, 19, 20, 34, 36, 42
  nobles of the, 39, 42
  offerings of the, 10, 20, 38, 44, 46,
    49, 50
  priests of the, 10, 34, 38, 45–47
  roadways of the, 32
  sacrifices of the, 10, 19–21, 26, 28,
    38, 42, 44, 50
  women of the, 24, 25, 50
Inti (sun god), 40
Inti Raimi, 38, 39

Johns Hopkins University, 26
Joy plaza, 39
Juanita (ice maiden), 29, 30
  care and study of, 16, 22, 24, 27
  costume of, 26
  death of, 28, 32, 40, 50
  grave site of, 19, 21
  sacrificing of, 36, 42, 45–47
  transporting corpse of, 12–14

lightning, 17, 19, 20, 40
Lima, Peru, 47
Llama Mama, 40
llamas, 10, 16, 19, 30, 38, 40, 42–46,
    49
lliclla, 24, 26
Lloque Yupanqui, 30
looters and treasure seekers, 12

Mama Ocllo, 29
Mama Quilla, 40
Manco Capac, 29, 36
Mount Aconcagua corpse, 44
Mount Ampato, 7, 9, 16, 45
Mount Copiapó, 17
Mount Sabancaya, 7, 12
mountains, honoring of, 40–42,
    49
mummies, 10(12, 22, 23, 38, 40
mummy bundle (fardo), 10, 20

Napa, 38
neolithic people, 14
Nova, 50

Pacha Kuyuchik, 40
pachaca chunca camayoc, 34
Pachachuti, 30
pack animals, 19
Pizarro, Francisco, 47
pottery, 10, 19, 46
Punchao, 38

Quechua, 49
quinoa, 34
quipu, 39

Reinhard, Johan, 7, 8, 10–13, 16, 17,
    19, 21, 28, 49, 50

Sajama, 40
sandals, 20, 44, 50
Sara Sara Mountain, 50
sara, 34
sarita, 50
Sora Mama, 40
South America, 10, 30, 44
Spanish conquistadors, 14, 30, 41, 47
spondylus shell, 8, 10
statuettes, 11, 24. *See also* figurines
Sun Temple, 38

Tata Sabaya, 40
tupu, 24, 25, 50

ukuku, 49

Viracocha, 29, 42
viruses and diseases, 11, 44, 48
volcanoes, 40

weapons, 14

Yahur Huaccac, 30

Zárate, Miguel, 7, 8, 10–13, 16, 18, 19

A B O U T   T H E   A U T H O R

Janet Buell is an elementary school enrichment teacher. Her main interests are anthropology, archaeology, reading, soccer, and softball. The time she spent exploring a local bog made her want to find out more. In her research, she discovered the existence of bog bodies and other ancient humans. It soon turned into the idea for this book series.

Janet was born and raised in Illinois and now lives in Goffstown, New Hampshire.